WAYS OF ATTENDING

Attention is not just receptive, but actively creative of the world we inhabit. How we attend makes all the difference to the world we experience. And nowadays in the West we generally attend in a rather unusual way: governed by the narrowly focused, target-driven left hemisphere of the brain.

Forget everything you thought you knew about the difference between the hemispheres, because it will be largely wrong. It is not what each hemisphere does – they are both involved in everything – but how it does it that matters. And the prime difference between the brain hemispheres is the manner in which they attend. For reasons of survival we need one hemisphere (in humans and many animals, the left) to pay narrow attention to detail, to grab hold of things we need, while the other, the right, keeps an eye out for everything else. The result is that one hemisphere is good at utilising the world, the other better at understanding it.

Absent, present, detached, engaged, alienated, empathic, broad or narrow, sustained or piecemeal, attention has the power to alter whatever it meets. The play of attention can both create and destroy, but it never leaves its object unchanged. How you attend to something – or don't attend to it – matters a very great deal. This book helps you to see what it is you may have been trained by our very unusual culture not to see.

Dr Iain McGilchrist is a Quondam Fellow of All Souls College, Oxford, a Fellow of the Royal College of Psychiatrists, a Fellow of the Royal Society of Arts, and former Consultant Psychiatrist and Clinical Director at the Bethlem Royal &

Maudsley Hospital, London. He was a Research Fellow in neuroimaging at Johns Hopkins Hospital, Baltimore, and a Fellow of the Institute of Advanced Studies in Stellenbosch. He has published original articles and research papers in a wide range of publications on topics in literature, medicine, and psychiatry. He is the author of *Against Criticism* (Faber, 1982), *The Master and his Emissary: The Divided Brain and the Making of the Western World* (Yale, 2009), T*he Divided Brain and the Search for Meaning: Why Are We So Unhappy?* (e-book short) and is currently working on a book of epistemology and metaphysics entitled *There Are No Things*, to be published by Penguin Press.

WAYS OF ATTENDING

How Our Divided Brain Constructs the World

Iain McGilchrist

Routledge
Taylor & Francis Group

LONDON AND NEW YORK

This is an edited version of an article that originally appeared in the Scientific and Medical Network Review and is reproduced by kind permission of the author and the Scientific and Medical Network (www.scimednet.org).

First published 2019
by Routledge
2 Park Square, Milton Park, Abingdon, Oxon OX14 4RN

and by Routledge
711 Third Avenue, New York, NY 10017

Routledge is an imprint of the Taylor & Francis Group, an informa business

British Library Cataloguing in Publication Data

A catalogue record for this book is available from the British Library

Library of Congress Cataloging-in-Publication Data

A catalog record has been requested for this book

ISBN: 978–0–429–43567–6 (ebk)
ISBN: 978–1–78181–533–5 (pbk)

Edited, designed, and typeset in Arial and Georgia
by Communication Crafts, East Grinstead

CONTENTS

CONTENTS

ABOUT THE AUTHOR

Dr Iain McGilchrist is a Quondam Fellow of All Souls College, Oxford, a Fellow of the Royal College of Psychiatrists, a Fellow of the Royal Society of Arts, and former Consultant Psychiatrist and Clinical Director at the Bethlem Royal & Maudsley Hospital, London. He was a Research Fellow in neuroimaging at Johns Hopkins Hospital, Baltimore, and a Fellow of the Institute of Advanced Studies in Stellenbosch. He has published original articles and research papers in a wide range of publications on topics in literature, medicine, and psychiatry. He is the author of *Against Criticism* (Faber, 1982), *The Master and his Emissary: The Divided Brain and the Making of the Western World* (Yale, 2009), T*he Divided Brain and the Search for Meaning: Why Are We So Unhappy?* (e-book short) and is currently working on a book of epistemology and metaphysics entitled *There Are No Things*, to be published by Penguin Press.

EDITOR'S NOTE

> Attention may sound a bit boring, but it isn't at all. It is not just another "cognitive function" – it is actually nothing less than the way in which we relate to the world. [Iain McGilchrist, *Ways of Attending*]

In this compelling introduction to his work, Iain McGilchrist unpacks one of the key concepts of his groundbreaking exploration of brain lateralization and its impact on human culture, *The Master and his Emissary: The Divided Brain and the Making of the Western World* (McGilchrist, 2009). The book is widely regarded as one of the most important and influential texts of the twenty-first century, a work of "absolutely crucial cultural and intellectual importance", as Professor Louis Sass has observed.

Central to McGilchrist's approach is the notion of attention. As he suggests, "attention is not just another 'function' alongside other cognitive functions". Rather, the kind of attention we bring to bear on the world actually alters the nature of the world we attend to: "Attention changes *what kind of* a thing comes into being for us: in that way it changes the world" (2009, p. 28). This transformative or "world-changing" aspect of attention can be seen in every form of relationship we encounter and experience – from parenting and teaching, to therapy, art, philosophy, science and political engagement. Adjusting our mode of attention can have far-reaching and profound effects – indeed, one might call this striking ability *"the attention effect"* , as remarkable a phenomenon in its way as the recognition in quantum mechanics of how the act of observation alters what is being observed.

As below, so above: the theologian Jacob Needleman has presciently noted that "the quality of man's attention is the key to the meaning of our lives and the possible growth of our being" (2009, p. 204). This is because *"I am my attention.* Everything else is given, is not *mine"* (p. 205). The unique role of attention has also been recognised in the new digital technologies of the modern "attention economy", in which the human gaze is increasingly being monetarised and mined as a resource, again pointing to its central position in the landscape of the twenty-first century. As content producers compete to capture our attention and emotional engagement, "this battle for attention creates what tech ethicist Tristan Harris has called 'a race to the bottom of the brain stem'" (Rose-Stockwell, 2017).

The left and right hemispheres of the brain play a vital, pivotal role in all this because they mediate and deliver – indeed embody – two discrete and distinct modes of attention. As McGilchrist (2009) observes, "each hemisphere attends to the world in a different way—and the ways are consistent" (p. 27): "My thesis is that for us as human beings there are two fundamentally opposed realities, two different modes of experience; that each is of ultimate importance in bringing about the recognisably human world; and that their difference is rooted in the bihemispheric structure of the brain" (p. 3). In a world that has become increasingly dominated by one particular mode of attention, one rooted in and promoted by the left hemisphere of the brain, consciously altering our habitual mode of attention to one based on a more integrated, empathic, relational and embodied sense of relationship can have dramatic, perhaps even revolutionary, consequences.

What is so striking about McGilchrist's work, apart from its extraordinary scope and subtlety of analysis, is how deftly it integrates these two distinct forms of engagement itself, capturing and reflecting in the very structure of his argument the function he is describing – interweaving neuroscience with the humanities, the internal with the external, combining detailed and precise analysis with a broad and immensely rich cultural and contextual framework. In this respect, the book is itself a remarkable embodiment of our two distinct ways of attending.

The present work explores the key themes and concerns of McGilchrist's work in as open and accessible form as possible. For this reason, academic referencing has been kept to a minimum: full references and clinical illustrations of the points can be found in *The Master and his Emissary*.

Rod Tweedy

Introduction

There's a story somewhere in Nietzsche that goes something like this. There was once a wise spiritual master, who was the ruler of a small but prosperous domain, and who was known for his selfless devotion to his people. As his people flourished and grew in number, the bounds of this small domain spread, and with it the need to trust implicitly the emissaries he sent to ensure the safety of its ever more distant parts. It was not just that it was impossible for him to order all that needed to be dealt with personally: as he wisely saw, he *needed* to keep his distance from, and even to remain ignorant of, such concerns. And so he nurtured and trained his emissaries carefully, in order that they could be trusted. Eventually, however, his cleverest and most ambitious vizier, the one he most trusted to do his work, began to see himself as the master and used his position to advance his own wealth and influence. He saw his master's temperance and forbearance as weakness, not wisdom, and on his missions on the master's behalf adopted his mantle as his own: the emissary became contemptuous of his master. And so it came about that the master was usurped, the people were duped, the domain became a tyranny, and eventually it collapsed in ruins.

This story is as old as humanity, and I think it tells us something important about what is going on inside ourselves, in our very brains. It is being played out in the world around us right now, and, since the consequences are grave indeed, we need to understand what it is.

The Master
and his Emissary

The story of the relationship between the structure of the brain and its influence on Western culture was the subject of my 2009 book, *The Master and his Emissary: The Divided Brain and the Making of the Western World*. I will try here to give an idea of how this book came about, since it may be of interest to those outside the world of neuroscience.

The idea of writing it goes back to the time before I even started training in medicine, more than 25 years ago. I had been troubled by problems of the academic study of literature, which was my business at the time: why was it that the things we prized about the work of a great poet, for example, turned to a handful of dust when one tried to inspect them more closely? On analysis and explicit discussion, the uniqueness of the work, which lay in these very same much-valued qualities, seemed to consist only of imperfections. I began to think less well of perfection. The whole process of literary criticism seemed inevitably to involve making explicit what had to remain implicit (if it was not to be seriously disrupted), substituting general words and thoughts that one might have got almost anywhere else for the irreducible uniqueness of the work of art and replacing the incarnate being before us with a series of abstractions – a coded message of which the author was unaware. We cerebralised what had to remain the "betweenness" of two living things. The result was a sort of superior knowingness that traduced the innocence of the work. Something often of undeniable interest emerged, but it nonetheless, subtly, missed the point altogether.

The crux seemed to be a misunderstanding of what is *embodied*, both in us and in the work of art, in the world we bring about for ourselves. I studied what was then thought of as the "mind–body problem" but found the philosophers too disembodied in their approach. (I had not yet come across the European philosophers – particularly Merleau-Ponty – who were aware of this difficulty and made it the centre of their work; such philosophers were ignorantly ignored in Oxford in those days.) I decided to train in medicine and get, as far as was possible, first-hand *experience* of how the brain and the body actually affect the mind, and how the mind affects the brain and the body.

After my training I went to the Maudsley, where, in 1990, I had the good fortune to hear John Cutting lecture on the right hemisphere of the brain, a subject on which he could fairly be said to be a world authority and on which he had just published an important book. I was amazed. I had been taught that – as one leading neuroscientist put it – the right hemisphere was about as gifted as a chimpanzee. But it turned out, on the basis, not of speculation, but of painstaking observation of what happened to people when something went wrong with the right hemisphere, that it was crucial to

4

just about everything we are and do – which is why the prospects for subjects with right-hemisphere damage are worse than for those with left-hemisphere damage, even though for most people loss of left-hemisphere function affects their speech and the use of their primary hand. It also turned out that the right hemisphere had a capacity the left hemisphere lacked for understanding the implicit, for appreciating uniqueness, for the embodied rather than the purely conceptual, for the ambiguous rather than the certain. There was even evidence that the left hemisphere had a more confident, superior attitude to whatever formed its "subject" than the right. Might this have some bearing on my dissatisfaction with the process of literary criticism? I set about gathering information.

The difference
between the hemispheres

Some of you may already be thinking: not the old chestnut about the hemispheres again, surely? Despite frequent acknowledgment by many leading neuroscientists that there do seem to be fundamental differences between the hemispheres, and despite some tantalising glimpses, scientists have largely given up trying to put their finger on what these might be, piece after piece of information showing that every conceivable activity – language, visual imagery, and all the things we thought in the past distinguished right from left – is served by *both* hemispheres, not just one. The problem is that we generally look at the brain as having "functions", and if you do that, sure enough, those functions are shared by both hemispheres. But if you look, not at what the brain does, as if it were just a machine, but at how – in the sense of "in what manner" – it does it, as if it were part of a living person, some very important differences start to emerge, and a picture begins to take shape that tells us some astonishing things about ourselves and our world. My view is that the relationship between the hemispheres, like that of the master and his emissary in the story, is not symmetrical. Each needs the other; each has an important role to play.

But those roles are not equal – one depends more on the other and needs to be aware of that fact. So I am not going to argue anything as facile as that the left hemisphere is "mistaken" in what it sees or what it values. It is not: but its vision is necessarily limited. The problem comes with its unawareness of that fact.

The first question has to be: why is the brain divided at all? If the whole purpose of the brain is to make connections, and if, as many believe, consciousness arises, in some yet to be specified manner, from the sheer interconnectedness of such a vast array of neurones, why chop it down the middle? It could have evolved as a single mass. But, in fact, hemisphere divisions go right down the phylogenetic tree. So whatever it is for, it must operate, not just for man, but also for animals and birds. What is that?

And, taking a closer look at the brain, why is it that the human brain is asymmetrical? There is a bump on the left side towards the back, which has traditionally been associated with the development of language. What is less well known is that there is a bump at the front on the right, too, as if the brain had been given a fairly sharp tweak clockwise from below. What on earth is that about?

Well, the bump on the left is already more of a puzzle than it seems. In the first place, it can't just be that in man language needed to be all in one place and, having to be *somewhere*, just happened to set up residence in the left hemisphere, where it caused the cortex to expand. For a start, as neuroscience has explained to us, everything – and that includes language – goes on in both hemispheres. Important aspects of language are served by the right hemisphere, too, so it can't be a matter of keeping it all "under one roof". In any case, it turns out that chimps and the great apes in general also have this bump on the left, even though they lack language in the human sense. And examination of the skulls of humans from long before language developed also show it. So it must be for something else. What was that?

You may say, "it's not about anything – it's just one of those things". But that would be a very odd finding. In nature structure and function go hand in hand. A good example is that in songbirds the left hemisphere (their "speech" centre) expands during the mating season and then contracts again when they stop singing once it is over. And the right hippocampus, where we store what we know about visuospatial exploration of the environment, grows larger in London cabbies when they take "the Knowledge". So we should assume that structure has meaning in terms of function.

Perhaps it has to do with handedness, then. But why do we have handedness at all? Skill acquisition is not like putting books on a shelf: that the more are put on one end, the more they will fall off the other. No, we could have had two equally skilful hands. And once again, while apes do have the left-sided bump, they don't exhibit handedness in the same way as we do – so it cannot be that, either. The plot thickens when you realise that the relative advantage of the left hemisphere/right hand is not, after all, the result of an overall increase in function in the left hemisphere, but of a *deliberate handicapping* of the right. There are several strands of research that demonstrate that quite clearly. It looks as if our conventional explanations just don't stand up.

Equally clearly, language and dominance of the right hand, now that we have them, are remarkably closely associated in the left hemisphere, and they have a great deal in common. For example, we use them both to *grasp* things, as we say. They must play a part in the story: it's just that they cannot be the cause. That must lie elsewhere, and language and handedness must be the "symptoms", rather than the explanation, of hemisphere differences.

The divided brain
and the evolution of language

If we come to look at the evolution of language, we find further puzzles. Why do we have language at all? Surely, in order to communicate. And if not that, then at least to think. But neither of these propositions is true.

The fact that humans can speak is dependent on the evolution, not just of the brain, but of the articulating apparatus – the larynx, the tongue and so on – and of respiratory control. That is why birds can imitate human speech, whereas apes, our nearest relatives, cannot: birds have the necessary equipment, in order to be able to sing. Through some fascinating detective work we can tell from looking at human skeletons when it was that the necessary developments in control of the tongue and larynx, and of the muscles of respiration, developed. That turns out to be from a time long before – from other evidence – we believe we developed language. So what were these developments for?

The answer, according to many anthropologists, appears to have been: in order to sing. That might sound odd, because we are used to thinking of music as a bit peripheral. But in fact the "music" of speech – in the sense of the intonation and all that is not "just" the content, coupled with other forms of non-verbal communication – constitutes the majority of what it is we communicate, when we do. Denotative language is not necessary for I–thou communication. Music is largely right-hemisphere-dependent, and the aspects of speech that enable us truly to understand the meaning of an utterance at a higher level – including intonation, irony, metaphor, and the meaning of an utterance in context – are still served by the right hemisphere. Denotative language becomes necessary when we have projects: when we need to communicate about a third party, or about things that are not present at the time. It expands immeasurably our capacity for manipulation – what one might call "I–it" communication. It is therefore, necessary, not for communication in itself, but for a certain *kind* of communication. Equally, there is a mass of evidence that we do not need language to think, even to conceptualise. One rather wonderful example is that, believe it or not, pigeons can distinguish between a Picasso and a Monet, without having any language in which to do it (Cerella, 1980; Matsukawa, Inoue, & Jitsumori, 2004; Watanabe, Sakamoto, & Wakita, 1995). But we also know that tribes that do not have numbers above "three" can calculate perfectly well to much larger numbers and have a grasp of concepts they cannot put into words. Language is not necessary for thinking, just for certain *kinds* of thinking. What was it for, then?

My view is that language and the hand have a certain common agenda – that is, they enable us to *grasp* things: to pin them down and make them useful. And we cannot deny that they have done that in spades. They have helped us to use the world and, by doing so, to develop many of the things of which we are most justly proud, the fruits of civilisation. But there is a price for this kind of approach to the world, and that brings us back to the question why the hemispheres are separated.

The nature
of attention

Let's go back to birds and what we call the lower animals. What do we know about hemisphere differences there? The first thing one can say is that they seem to underwrite different kinds of attention. Attention may sound a bit boring, but it isn't at all. It is not just another "cognitive function" – it is actually nothing less than the way in which we relate to the world. And it doesn't just dictate the *kind* of relationship we have with whatever it is: it dictates *what it is that we come to have a relationship with*.

In order to stay alive, birds have to solve a conundrum: they need to be able to feed and watch out for predators simultaneously. How are you to focus closely on what you are doing when you are trying to pick out that grain of seed from the grit on which it lies while, at the same time, keeping the broadest possible open attention to whatever may be, in order to avoid being eaten? It's a bit like trying to pat your head while rubbing your stomach at the same time – only worse, because it is impossible. What we know is that the difference in attention between the hemispheres makes the apparently impossible possible. Birds pay narrowly focused attention with their right eye (left hemisphere) to what they are eating, while keeping their left eye (right hemisphere) open for predators. At the same time, birds and animals use their left eye (right hemisphere) in forming bonds with others of their kind. And this difference is preserved as we evolve. In fact, it seems that the left hemisphere specialises in a sort of piecemeal attention that helps us to make use of the world, but in doing so it alters our relationship with it. Equally, the right hemisphere subserves a broad, open attention that enables us to see ourselves connected to – and, in the human case, to empathise with – whatever is other than ourselves.

These kinds of attention are mutually incompatible, though we need to be able to employ both simultaneously. In humans, because of the development of the frontal lobes, which enable us to stand back from the world, the need for specialisation becomes greater. As we stand back, we can see the world either as separate from ourselves, as something we can *use*, or as quite the opposite – as connected to ourselves more deeply: we can see others, for the first time, as beings like ourselves, the ground of empathy. Being able to represent the world artificially – to map it conceptually, substituting tokens for things, like the general's map at army HQ – enables us to have an overall strategy; and this is what language achieves. But it inhibits us from being *there*, in the experiential world. It places us at one remove from things. So for humans the need to have both ways of understanding the world, and yet keeping them apart, is paramount. And it turns out that in humans the corpus callosum, the band of tissue that connects the hemispheres, while it does both connect and inhibit, is more involved with the process of inhibition, with keeping things separate.

What is the left-hemisphere expansion in apes for, then? It has to do with their capacity to form concepts, in order the better to manipulate the world. And so it is in humans, where it is also related to our capacity for language and, literally, to manipulation with the right hand. And the bump at the front on the right in humans, and in some apes, is associated with a whole array of "functions" that distinguish us from other animals and relate to our capacity for empathy: in intimate connection with the right hemisphere as a whole, it plays a significant part in imagination, creativity, the capacity for religious awe, music, dance, poetry, art, love of nature, a moral sense, a sense of humour and the ability to change our minds. The ways in which hemisphere differences affect what each hemisphere "does" are profound.

Unfortunately, though the hemispheres need to cooperate, they find themselves in competition, simply because the left hemisphere's take on things is such that it thinks it knows it all, while it *cannot* be aware of what the right hemisphere knows. Each needs the other, but the left hemisphere is more dependent on the right than the right is on the left. Yet it thinks exactly the opposite and believes that it can "go it alone". I believe the battle between the hemispheres (which is only a battle from the left hemisphere's point of view) explains the shape of the history of ideas in the West and explains the predicament we find ourselves in today.

How our divided brain constructs the world

Let's return to attention. As has been noted, attention is the basis of our experience of the world. It is not a "function" alongside other functions, but the foundation for having a world at all in which those "functions" can be exercised. And although it is true that what it is we are attending to determines the type of attention we pay to it, it is also importantly true that the type of attention we pay determines *what it is we see*. The way reality comes into being for us is like that famous picture by M C Escher of hands that draw hands:

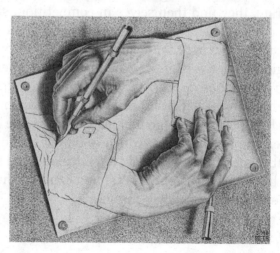

So what has the exponential growth in brain research over recent years actually revealed about hemisphere differences? And what sort of a world does each create for us? Here I am going to have to summarise in almost telegraphically compressed form what we know. All I can say is that the evidence is, in my view, both extensive and convincing, and those who are interested will find the relevant research given in detail in *The Master and his Emissary*.

As if to confirm that there is something quite distinct about the ways the hemispheres work, we might just note that there are differences in their structure and function at the most basic level. The right hemisphere is longer, wider, and generally larger as well as heavier than the left: a finding that applies to all social mammals.

The hemispheres also differ in their sensitivity to particular neurotransmitters and neurohormones, as well as in neuronal architecture and organisation, in ways that make sense in terms of their neuropsychological differences.

In the first place, the nature of right-hemisphere attention means that whatever we experience comes to us first – it "presences" to us in unpreconceived freshness – in the right hemisphere. New experience of all kinds – whether it be music, words, imaginary constructs, objects in the environment, even skills – comes to us first from the right hemisphere and is dealt with by the left hemisphere only later, once it becomes familiar.

The right hemisphere is better at making connections between things: it tends to see things whole, whereas the left hemisphere sees the parts. This has further consequences. The left hemisphere tends to see things more in the abstract, the right hemisphere sees them more embedded in the real-world context in which they occur. As a corollary, the right hemisphere seems better able to appreciate actually existing things in all their uniqueness, while the left hemisphere schematises and generalises things into categories. But since much of what matters in experience depends ultimately on not being snatched from the context in which alone it has meaning, this is a vastly significant difference. All artistic and spiritual experience – perhaps everything truly important – can only be implicit; language, in making things explicit, reduces everything to the same worn coinage and, as Nietzsche said, makes the uncommon common.

There is a mass of evidence that the left hemisphere is better attuned to tools and to whatever is inanimate, mechanical, machine-like, and which it itself has made: such things are understandable in their own terms, because they were put together by it, piece by piece, and they are ideally suited to this kind of understanding. In contrast, the right hemisphere is adapted to dealing with living things, which are flexible, organic, constantly changing, and which it has not made. The right hemisphere alone appears to be able to appreciate the organic wholeness of a flowing structure that changes over time, as in fact all living things are; and, indeed, almost all aspects of the appreciation of time are in the right hemisphere. By contrast, the left hemisphere sees time as a succession of points and sees flow as a succession of static moments, rather like the still frames of a ciné film. Everything, including living wholes, is put together from bits; and if there are no clear bits, it will invent them.

It is therefore not surprising that the right hemisphere is far more important than the left for the appreciation of music – which is organic, which flows, which needs to be appreciated as a whole, and which exists almost entirely in "betweenness". The left hemisphere can appreciate rhythm, as long as it is simple, but little else: melody, timbre, and, especially, harmony are all largely right-hemisphere-dependent, as are complex rhythms, with cross-beats and syncopations. (Professional musicians are an exception to this right-hemisphere dependency, for a number of possible reasons that are interesting in themselves – see *The Master and his Emissary*, p. 75.)

The visual equivalent of harmony could be said to be depth of the visual field; the sense of depth is also largely right-hemisphere-dependent, in keeping with the right hemisphere's world as one from which we are not isolated, but with which we stand in an important relationship. The left hemisphere, on the other hand, tends to see things as flat, detached from us, as though projected onto a screen.

While both hemispheres are involved in the expression and appreciation of emotion, the majority of our emotional life depends on the right hemisphere. The one emotion that is robustly demonstrated to be more associated with the left hemisphere is anger, though emotions that are superficial, conscious or willed may be subserved by the left hemisphere. We express more with the left side of the face, which is governed by the right hemisphere; the left hemisphere cannot read emotional facial expression or understand or remember emotional material as well as the right. In fact, the recognition of faces, discriminating their uniqueness, interpreting their expressions, are all largely dependent on the right hemisphere. Above all, the right hemisphere is more empathetic: its stance towards others is less competitive and more attuned to compassion and fellow feeling. Although it can deal well with the entire range of emotions, it is far better attuned to sadness than the left hemisphere. The close relatedness between empathy and the capacity for sadness has indeed been confirmed by studies in children.

The right hemisphere is more interested in what has personal relevance "for me", the left hemisphere in what is impersonal. But it is still the right hemisphere that is better able to understand what is going on in other people's heads, and to empathise, than the left hemisphere, which in these respects is relatively autistic. Our sense of our self is complex, but again the sense of ourselves as beings with a past and a future, as single beings with an enduring story over time, is dependent on the right hemisphere. (Narrative is appreciated by the right hemisphere, whereas the left hemisphere sees a mass of discrete episodes, which it often gets out of sequence.) The sense of ourselves as identified with our conscious will may be more subserved by the left hemisphere.

That our embodied nature enters into everything we do – not just our actions, or even our feelings, but our ability to reason, philosophise or engage in science – is something of which we have become more aware in the last hundred years. The hemispheres have different ways of understanding the body. Only the right hemisphere has a whole-body image; the left hemisphere sees the body as an assemblage of parts and as if it were an object in space alongside other objects, rather than a mode of existence. For the right hemisphere, we live the body; for the left, we live *in* it, rather as we drive a car.

Reasoning is by no means confined to the left hemisphere, though sequential analysis largely is. Deductive reasoning, many kinds of mathematical procedures and problem-solving, and the phenomenon of sudden insight into the nature of a complex construct seem to be underwritten by the right hemisphere – in fact, by areas that cognitive science tells us are also involved in the "processing" of emotion.

The intuitive moral sense is closely bound up with empathy for others and seems to depend on part of the right frontal cortex that is dysfunctional in psychopaths. Above all, the left hemisphere is over-optimistic and unrealistically positive in its self-appraisal; it is in denial about its short-comings, unreasonably certain that it understands things of which it has little knowledge, and disinclined to change its mind. By contrast, the right hemisphere sees more but is far more inclined to self-doubt, is more uncertain of what it knows – and it has no voice, since the motor speech centre (though, importantly, not all of language) lies in the left hemisphere.

If one had to characterise the difference overall, it is something like this. Experience is forever in motion, ramifying and unpredictable. In order for us to *know* anything at all, that thing must have enduring properties. If all things flow and one can never step into the same river twice – Heraclitus's phrase is, I believe, a brilliant evocation of the core reality of the right hemisphere's world – one will always be taken unawares by experience: since nothing is ever being repeated, nothing can ever be known. We have to find a way of fixing it as it flies, stepping back from the immediacy of experience, stepping outside the flow. Hence the brain has to attend to the world in two completely different ways, and in so doing to bring two different worlds into being. In the one, that of the right hemisphere, we *experience* the live, complex, embodied world of individual, always unique, beings, forever in flux, a net of interdependencies, forming and reforming wholes, a world with which we are deeply connected. In the other, that of the left hemisphere, we "experience" our experience in a special way: a "re-presented" version of it, containing now static, separable, bounded, but essentially fragmented entities, grouped into classes on which predictions can be based. This kind of attention isolates, fixes and makes each thing explicit by bringing it under the spotlight of attention. In doing so it renders things inert, mechanical, lifeless. But it also enables us for the first time to know, and consequently to learn and to make things. This gives us power.

These two aspects of the world are not symmetrically opposed. They are not equivalent, for example, to the "subjective" and "objective" points of view, concepts that are themselves a product of, and already reflect, one particular way of being in the world – which, in fact, importantly, already reflect a "view" of the world, such as only the left hemisphere can take. The distinction I am trying to make is between, on the one hand, the way in which we experience the world pre-reflectively, before we have had a chance to "view" it at all or to divide it up into bits – a world in which what has later come to be thought of as subjective and objective are held in a suspension that embraces each potential "pole" and their togetherness, together – and, on the other, the world we are more used to thinking of, in which subjective and objective appear as separate poles. At its simplest, a world where there is "betweenness", and one where there is not. These are not different ways of *thinking about* the world: they are different ways of *being in* the world. And their difference is not symmetrical, but fundamentally asymmetrical.

Above I suggested that we have developed language not for communication, not even for thinking, but to enable a certain type of functional manipulation of the world. Language is like the general's map at HQ: a *representation* of the world. It is no longer present, but literally "re-presented" after the fact. What it delivers is a useful fiction.

I believe the essential difference between the right hemisphere and the left hemisphere is that the right hemisphere pays attention to the Other: to whatever it is that exists apart from ourselves, with which it sees itself in profound relation. It is deeply attracted to, and given life by, the relationship, the betweenness, that exists with this Other. By contrast, the left hemisphere pays attention to the virtual world that it has created, which is self-consistent but self-contained, ultimately disconnected from the Other, making it powerful – but also curiously impotent, because it is ultimately only able to operate on, and to know, itself.

The primacy
of the right hemisphere

You might say: OK, here are two different ways of conceiving the world: but how do you know that they are not equally valid? I say that they are both very important – both, in fact, essential for our ability to lead civilised lives – but not equally valid. And there are many reasons for this.

In the first place, it is interesting that, in the late nineteenth and the twentieth centuries, both mathematics and physics (for example, Cantor, Boltzmann, Gödel, Bohr) and philosophy (I am here thinking particularly of the American pragmatists, Dewey and James, and the European phenomenologists, Husserl, Heidegger, Scheler, Merleau-Ponty and the later Wittgenstein), though starting absolutely from the premise of the left hemisphere that sequential analysis will lead us to the truth, have ended up with results that approximate far more closely – and in fact confirm the validity of – the right hemisphere's way of understanding the world, *not* that of the left. That is in itself a remarkable fact, since generally speaking the preconceptions with which you start will determine where you end.

But there are other indications. Broad vigilant attention must come before we can focus on one part of the field. We see the whole before we see the parts, rather than putting the whole together from the parts. We experience everything at first with the right hemisphere, not with the left. Language originates in the body and is implicit: it does not function at the abstract level, as something explicit. Affect is primary, not the result of calculation based on cognitive evaluation of the parts. As Libet (1985) has demonstrated, the unconscious will, more closely related to right-hemisphere functioning, is well ahead of anything our explicit verbalising consciousness can be aware of (Kornhuber & Decke, 1965). Careful analysis of the relationship between speech and gesture shows that both thought and its expression actually originate in the right hemisphere, not in the left. Re-presentation necessarily relies on earlier "presencing". And even the mode of functioning of the nervous system itself is more right-hemisphere-congruent than left-hemisphere-congruent.

What the left hemisphere offers is, then, a valuable but intermediate process, one of "unpacking" what is there and handing it back to the right hemisphere, where it can once again be integrated into the experiential whole, much as the painstaking fragmentation and analysis of a sonata in practice is reintegrated by the pianist in performance at a level where he or she must no longer be aware of it.

That, at any rate, is how the two should work together: the emissary reporting back to the master, who alone can see the broader picture. But the self-consistent rationalism of the left hemisphere has convinced it that it does not need to concern itself with what the right hemisphere knows: it believes it has the whole story itself. And it has three great advantages. First, it has control of the voice and the means of argument: the three Ls – language, logic and linearity – are all ultimately under left-hemisphere control. It is like being the Berlusconi of the brain: a political heavyweight who has control of the media. Of course we tend to listen more to what it has to say. Second, the self-consistent world of pure theory and ideas is like a hall of mirrors: all attempts to escape are deflected back within. The main paths that might have led us to something beyond – the intuitive wisdom embodied in tradition, the experience of the natural world, arts, the body and religion – are all emptied of force by the abstracting, rationalising, ironising impact of the world of self-consistent re-presentations that is yielded by the left hemisphere. The living presence is no longer accessible. And, third, there is a tendency for positive feedback to come into play: instead of redressing the balance, we just get more of the same.

Which brings me to the reason we cannot just view this as of academic interest. For I believe the world in which we live has come increasingly to reflect the view of the left hemisphere alone.

The triumph
of the left hemisphere

In the second part of *The Master and his Emissary* ("How the Brain Has Shaped Our World"), I look at the evolution of Western culture, beginning in the ancient world with the extraordinary efflorescence of culture in sixth-century-BC Athens, where, it seems to me, the two hemispheres worked in harmony as never before or since; then at the decline associated with the rise of the left hemisphere in the late Roman empire; and then, in turn, at the seismic shifts that we call the Renaissance, the Reformation, the Enlightenment, Romanticism, the Industrial Revolution, Modernism and Post-modernism. I believe that they represent a power struggle between these two ways of experiencing the world, and that we have ended up prisoners of just one – that of the left hemisphere alone.

Let's do a thought experiment. What would it look like if the left hemisphere came to be the sole purveyor of our reality?

First of all, the whole picture would be unattainable: the world would become a heap of bits. Its only meaning would come through its capacity to be used. More narrowly focused attention would lead to an increasing specialisation and technicalising of knowledge. This, in turn, would promote the substitution of information, and information gathering, for knowledge, which comes through experience. Knowledge, in its turn, would seem more "real" than what one might call wisdom, which would seem too nebulous, something never to be grasped. Knowledge that has come through experience, and the practical acquisition of embodied skill, would become suspect, appearing either a threat or simply incomprehensible. It would be replaced by tokens or representations – formal systems, to be evidenced by paper qualifications.

There would be a simultaneous increase in both abstraction and reification, whereby the human body itself, and we ourselves, as well as the material world and the works of art we have created to understand it, would both become more conceptual and yet be seen as mere things. The world as a whole would become more virtualised and our experience of it would be increasingly through meta-representations of one kind or another; fewer people would find themselves doing work involving contact with anything in the real, "lived" world, rather than with plans, strategies, paperwork, management and bureaucratic procedures.

There would be a complete loss of the sense of uniqueness. Increasingly, the living would be modelled on the mechanical. This would also have an effect on the way bureaucracies would deal with human situations and with society at large. "Either/or" would tend to be substituted for matters of degree, and a certain inflex-ibility would result.

There would be a derogation of higher values and a cynicism about their status. Morality would come to be judged at best on the basis of utilitarian calculation, at worst on the basis of enlightened self-interest.

The impersonal would come to replace the personal. There would be a focus on material things at the expense of the living. Social cohesion and the bonds between person and person – and, just as importantly, between person and place, the context in which each person belongs – would be neglected, perhaps actively disrupted, as both inconvenient and incomprehensible to the left hemisphere acting on its own. There would be a depersonalisation of the relationships between members of society, and in society's relationship with its members. Exploitation rather than cooperation would, explicitly or not, be the default relationship between human individuals and between humanity and the rest of the world. Resentment would lead to an emphasis on uniformity and equality, not as just one desirable to be balanced with others, but as the ultimate desirable, transcending all others.

The left hemisphere cannot trust and is prone to paranoia. It needs to feel in control. We would expect government to become obsessed with issues of security above all else, and to seek total control.

Reasonableness would be replaced by rationality, and perhaps the very concept of reasonableness might become unintelligible. There would be a complete failure of common sense, since it is intuitive and relies on both hemispheres working together. One would expect a loss of insight, coupled with an unwillingness to take responsibility, and this would reinforce the left hemisphere's tendency to a perhaps dangerously unwarranted optimism. There would be a rise in intolerance and inflexibility, an unwillingness to change track or to change one's mind.

We would expect there to be a resentment of – and a deliberate undercutting of – the sense of awe or wonder: Weber's "disenchanted" world. Religion would seem to be mere fantasy. Art would be conceptualised, cerebralised; beauty would be ironised out of existence.

As a culture, we would come to discard tacit forms of knowing altogether. There would be a remarkable difficulty in understanding non-explicit meaning and a downgrading of non-verbal, non-explicit communication. Concomitant with this would be a rise in explicitness, backed up by ever-increasing legislation – what de Tocqueville predicted as a "network of small complicated rules" that would eventually strangle democracy (de Tocqueville, 2003, pp. 723–724). As it became less possible to rely on a shared and intuitive moral sense or on implicit contracts between individuals, such rules would grow ever more burdensome. There would be less tolerance for and appreciation of the value of ambiguity. We would tend to be over-explicit in the language we use to approach art and religion, accompanied by a loss in their vital, implicit, metaphorical power.

Does that ring any bells? In terms of the fable with which I began, the emissary, insightless as ever, appears to believe it can see everything, do everything, alone. But it cannot: on its own it is like a zombie, a sleep-walker ambling straight towards the abyss, whistling a happy tune.

REFERENCES

Cerella, J. (1980). The pigeon's analysis of pictures. *Pattern Recognition, 12* (1): 1–6.

Cutting, J. (1990). *The Right Cerebral Hemisphere and Psychiatric Disorders.* Oxford: Oxford University Press.

de Tocqueville, A. (2003). *Democracy in America*, trans. H. Reeve & E. W. Plaag. New York: Barnes & Noble.

Kornhuber, H. H., & Decke, L. (1965). Hirnpotentialänderungen bei Willkürbewegungen und passiven Bewegungen des Menschen: Bereitschaftspotential und reafferente Potentiale. *Pflügers Archiv European Journal of Physiology, 284*: 1–17.

Libet, B. (1985). Unconscious cerebral initiative and the role of the conscious will in voluntary action. *Behavioural and Brain Sciences, 8* (4): 529–539.

Matsukawa, A., Inoue , S., & Jitsumori M. (2004). Pigeon's recognition of cartoons: Effects of fragmentation, scrambling, and deletion of elements. *Behavioural Processes, 65* (1): 25–34.

McGilchrist, I. (2009). *The Master and his Emissary: The Divided Brain and the Making of the Western World.* New Haven, CT: Yale University Press.

Needleman, J. (2009). *What Is God?* New York: Penguin.

Rose-Stockwell, T. (2017). This is how your fear and outrage are being sold for profit: The story of how one metric has changed the way you see the world. *The Mission*, 15 July 2017. https://medium.com/the-mission/the-enemy-in-our-feeds-e86511488de

Watanabe, S., Sakamoto J., & Wakita, M. (1995). Pigeons' discrimination of paintings by Monet and Picasso. *Journal of the Experimental Analysis of Behaviour, 63* (2): 165–174.

Printed in the United States
by Baker & Taylor Publisher Services